D0459206

SHOCK ZONE™

DEADLY AND DANGEROUS

DEADLY

Hard-Hitting

SPORTS

JEFF SAVAGE

Lerner Publications Company • Minneapolis

Lerner Publications Company
A division of Lerner Publishing Group, Inc.
241 First Avenue North
Minneapolis, MN 55401 U.S.A.

Website address: www.lernerbooks.com

Library of Congress Cataloging-in-Publication Data

Savage, Jeff.
    Deadly hard-hitting sports / by Jeff Savage.
        p.   cm. — (Shockzone™—deadly and dangerous)
    Includes index.
    ISBN 978–1–4677–0602–5 (lib. bdg. : alk. paper)
        1. Endurance sports. I. Title.
    GV749.5.S38 2013
    613.7'1—dc23   2012022492

Manufactured in the United States of America
1 – PC – 12/31/12

TABLE OF CONTENTS

Sure, injuries are a part of sports. But would you play a sport in which the injury can be *lethal*? **We're talking about the ultimate injury—death.** There's no bigger loss in sports than that! Is competing in such a sport worth that risk? To some people, it is. They know the hazards. They've heard the stories. They've read the statistics. Yet they participate anyway. They do so for the thrill and challenge.

If you decide to take up some of these sports, you might not live long enough to play chess when you're old and gray!

You already know some of the sports in this book. Others you will learn about for the first time. Some of the details you read will be gruesome. Can you imagine being crushed inside your race car or splattered on a sidewalk? After you finish reading, ask yourself: Would you be willing to risk your life to try one of these sports? Do you have the stomach for it?

Street Luging

You're rolling downhill on a board with wheels at 60 miles (97 kilometers) per hour. You're flat on your back, just inches off the ground. You have no brakes. Good luck!

Street luging is an extreme sport that can turn deadly in an instant. You are powered by gravity. The steeper the road, the faster you go. Much like a skateboard, you turn by leaning. One false move means road rash or broken bones—or worse.

Street luge was born in the 1970s, with California kids lying down on their skateboards and "butt-boarding" down hills. In 1975 the U.S. Skateboard Association held the first professional race. Street luge became part of the X Games in 1995. There are other contests worldwide.

Lugers race side by side to the finish line. A luge board is sometimes called a sled. It is about 5 feet (1.5 meters) long and usually made of aluminum, fiberglass, or wood. Lugers wear a hard-shell helmet and leather racing suit and gloves. Such protection sometimes isn't enough.

fiberglass = reinforced plastic material

Many street lugers on open roads have been killed. Most deaths occur at a turn in the road. Riders are going faster than they should and cannot turn sharply enough. They go off course and strike an object like a guardrail, a post, or a tree. Competition courses are often lined with safety barriers such as hay bales. But no course is completely safe, and it is the danger of luge that thrills competitors and fans alike.

BOXING

Since 1950 there have been about 550 deaths from boxing. That averages to about nine deaths per year, or one every six weeks. Not all boxing matches end in misery. But boxing is a violent and sometimes tragic sport. Why wouldn't it be? After all, the goal is to punch your opponent as hard as you can, as many times as you can, until you knock him out or the referee stops the fight.

How does the referee know when to stop a fight? A boxer might have trouble keeping his balance. His eyes might appear glazed. In later rounds, his neck may weaken. At this point, a hard punch can snap a boxer's head back, causing his brain to crash into his skull. This can result in a concussion or worse.

concussion =
a brain injury
that changes the
way the brain
functions

Padded gloves and headgear protect these amateur boxers from serious injuries.

In the past, boxing matches didn't have many rules. Boxers used to fight bare-fisted. They threw punches until one of the fighters gave up or was knocked out. There was no limit to the number of rounds in a fight.

Officials have tried to make boxing safer. In recent years, of course, boxers wear padded gloves. Referees receive better training and stop fights more quickly. Matches end after a certain number of rounds, even if the referee doesn't stop the fight first. But tragedy still strikes.

SEVENTY-FIVE ROUNDS!?

Bare-fisted boxing has been illegal in the United States for more than one hundred years. An official bare-fisted boxing match was last held in the United States in 1889. John L. Sullivan, known as the Boston Strong Man, took on Jake Kilrain in Richburg, Mississippi. The two fighters slugged it out in round after round. Finally, Kilrain's corner threw in the towel to end the fight—after seventy-five rounds!

Today, referees make sure a fighter's health isn't in danger before letting the match continue.

The most infamous death occurred in 1982. Ray "Boom Boom" Mancini was the lightweight boxing champion of the world. Duk Koo Kim was the challenger. Fans filled the outdoor stadium near Caesars Palace in Las Vegas to see this title fight. Millions more watched on television. The boxers battled into the fourteenth round. Kim had never fought for so many rounds as a professional. He was exhausted.

Mancini hit Kim with a powerful right hand. Kim collapsed to the canvas. He tried to pull himself to his feet, but the referee ended the fight and declared Mancini the winner. Minutes later, Kim collapsed again. He slipped into a coma. Emergency brain surgery was performed. Five days later, Kim died on his hospital bed.

This boxing bout ended with a knockout in the eighth round.

STOP ALREADY!
Duk Koo Kim's death has saved the lives of others. Most experts agreed that since Kim was so tired, he was more likely to suffer a deadly punch. Because of Kim's death, professional championship matches were reduced from fifteen rounds to twelve.

BASE JUMPING

Look! Up in the sky! Is it a bird? Is it a plane? No, it's a BASE jumper! This sport is so deadly that it is outlawed in most states. An estimated one out of every sixty people who jumps dies. But that doesn't stop everyone.

The term *BASE* stands for buildings, antennae, spans, and earth. Jumpers launch themselves from one of these platforms with a parachute. They hope to land safely. But sometimes they don't pull the parachute cord in time. Other times the parachute fails to open. In either case, the result is death.

No one knows who made the first BASE jump, but many in the sport point to an event in 1978 as its origin. It happened in Yosemite National Park atop a huge granite rock formation called El Capitan. Phil Smith and Phil Mayfield were the jumpers. Carl Boenish filmed the event. Smith and Mayfield fell about 3,000 feet (914 m) to safety. Later, they jumped from a radio tower and a bridge. In January 1981, they became the first to complete all four categories when they jumped from a skyscraper in Houston, Texas.

Smith and Mayfield were declared BASE 1 and BASE 2. BASE numbers have been awarded to jumpers ever since. As of 2013, more than fifteen hundred BASE numbers have been issued.

BASE JUMPING 101

earth = in BASE jumping, *earth* refers to cliffs and other tall rock formations

parachute = a blanket-sized device, usually made of nylon, that allows a person or object to land safely from a high fall

spans = bridges, ropeways, railroad trestles, and other things that extend from one high point to another

BASE jumping is eight times more deadly than skydiving from an airplane. Why? Because BASE jumps are usually made at much lower heights. Jumpers have only a few seconds to position their bodies and pull their parachute cords. For instance, a BASE jump from a height of 500 feet (152 m) allows a jumper just 5.6 seconds before striking the ground if his parachute does not open. If the jumper is tumbling or upside down and can't open his parachute in time, the result is likely fatal.

German BASE jumper Mirko Schmidt made his last jump in 2011—when he didn't pull his parachute chord in time.

BASE jumping is not always illegal. It is often featured in action movies, including several James Bond films. Organized competitions are held around the country, with accurate landings or free-fall tricks used to determine the winner. The most popular event is Bridge Day in Fayetteville, West Virginia. The New River Gorge Bridge spans 876 feet (267 m) above the river. Nearly five hundred jumpers compete each year. The event attracts more than one hundred thousand spectators.

RECORD FIRSTS AND MOSTS

- The first official test of a parachute by a person was believed to be in 1912, in Paris, France. Franz Reichelt had just invented a wearable parachute, and he tried it out by jumping from the Eiffel Tower. He died.

- In 2006 Captain Daniel G. Schilling set the record for the most BASE jumps in a twenty-four-hour period. Schilling jumped off a bridge in Twin Falls, Idaho, 201 times.

- Three women—Melody Morin, Ana Isabel Dao, and Anniken Binz—jumped from Venezuela's Angel Falls, the world's highest waterfall at 3,212 feet (979 m), in 2009.

CAVE DIVING

You're underwater in the Devil's Eye Cave in Florida. You're swimming through narrow tunnels, your air tank strapped to your back. You're breathing through your supply hose. You are frog kicking with your fins, hundreds of feet from the surface entrance. Suddenly the light attached to the back of your hand goes out. It's dark! You cannot reach your backup light. Now what?

Cave diving is a thrilling sport—until things go wrong. And deep underwater, plenty of things can go wrong. The society that oversees the sport says a successful cave dive is "one you return from."

A cave dive can last ninety minutes or more. In an emergency, a diver cannot swim up to the surface because of the cave's ceiling.

Instead, the diver must swim the entire way back to the entrance. And coming up too quickly from a dive can cause brain damage or death. That helps make the sport so deadly.

Another danger is running out of air. Smart divers practice the rule of thirds. One-third of a diver's air supply is used for entering a cave. One-third is for exiting, and one-third is to give to someone else in case of emergency.

Getting lost is another risk. To help prevent this, a guideline is attached to the cave entrance. The guideline is carried through the tunnels by the leader of a dive team. Unexpected water currents can pull a diver away from the group. Since 1960 more than five hundred people have died in cave diving accidents. But exploring water-filled caves is a challenge that some people just can't resist.

This diver needs to save enough air to get back out of the cave.

Freestyle Motocross

Travis Pastrana had suffered thirty broken bones and nine head injuries from motorcycle jumping. But that didn't stop him. At the 2006 Summer X Games in Los Angeles, Pastrana became the first rider to land a double backflip on a motorcycle. The trick was so dangerous that Pastrana vowed never to try it again. But he has tried it successfully several times since.

> double backflip = rotating 360 degrees backward two times in the air

In 2007 Scott Murray attempted the double backflip. He crashed and suffered a concussion. A few months later, Murray tried it again at an event in Italy. This time he landed it.

At the 2008 Summer X Games, Jim DeChamp attempted a front flip on his motorcycle. He crashed and suffered a broken back. Three months later, DeChamp returned. On the popular television show *Nitro Circus,* DeChamp attempted the front flip again. This time he was successful.

What keeps these riders coming back for more? They do it to push their limits and to dazzle the fans. Freestyle motocross (FMX) riders perform jumps and stunts to impress judges.

There are usually two FMX events. Standard freestyle takes place on a course with several jumps. Riders execute as many wild tricks as they can in a certain amount of time. Big Air is performing a single jump off a large dirt ramp. Riders soar 100 feet (30 m) through the air. People aren't built to fly, of course. So riders wear protective gear, including a helmet, gloves, boots, and a chest protector.

ISLE OF (THE DEAD) MAN

When it comes to racing, motorcycles are more deadly than cars. That's because driving fast on four wheels is more stable than riding on two. The deadliest motorcycle race in the world is the International Isle of Man Tourist Trophy Race. It is held each year on an island 32 miles (52 km) long and 14 miles (22 km) wide in the Irish Sea. Riders speed through rock-lined streets and narrow pathways on motorcycles that reach speeds up to 180 miles (290 km) per hour. More than 220 riders have been killed in the event.

FREE SOLO CLIMBING

You are clinging to a rock wall. You are 1,000 feet (305 m) above the ground. The pine trees below look like grass. You are hanging by your fingertips and your feet. You have nothing to catch you if you fall. Sound fun? To a free solo climber, it is!

Free solo climbing is the most dangerous form of rock climbing. It is also called free hand climbing. You climb alone, without a safety belt or other gear for protection. If you fall, you die.

There are many styles of rock climbing. In most styles, climbers use ropes and harnesses to keep from falling. Teams of climbers help one another and provide extra safety. Still, all forms of climbing are dangerous. An average of 113 people die each year from rock climbing.

Climbing a sheer rock face takes concentration. Water can seep from cracks, making the surface slippery. Any part of the rock can crumble. Every movement must be exact. Super strength is also required.

Alain Robert is known as the French Spider-Man for his ability to scale buildings and rock walls, sometimes using just his hands. Alex Honnold was featured on the television show *60 Minutes* for being the first to climb granite landmarks in Yosemite National Park. Amazing strength oozed from Honnold's fingertips. He could perform two-finger pull-ups, one arm at a time.

Most free solo climbers learn on a climbing wall. These indoor walls have a rocklike surface with grips for hands and feet. Once you master a climbing wall, you might be ready for free solo climbing outdoors—if you dare.

OLYMPIC MOVEMENT

The International Olympic Committee recognizes rock climbing with ropes and harnesses as a sport. It may soon be added to the Olympic Games.

Climbing Half Dome in Yosemite National Park can be deadly.

HELI-SKIING

Imagine riding in a helicopter over spectacular mountaintops. What could be more exciting? Picture skiing or snowboarding freely through fluffy white powder. If you're a heli-skier, you get to enjoy the thrill of both.

Heli-skiing is downhill skiing in the wilderness. Heli-boarding is using a snowboard instead. You can only reach these remote backcountry locations in a helicopter. There are no chairlifts and no cozy ski lodges. And there is no one to help you if something goes wrong. Once you and your group reach the top, you can glide down the mountain in any direction your guide chooses to take you. The adventure is delightful—until disaster strikes!

Mountain weather can change suddenly—and make a helicopter ride much more dangerous.

Heli-skiing can turn deadly in an instant. You can lose your footing and crash into a tree or slide off a cliff. You can drown in a creek bed that is hidden beneath the snow. A terrible storm can leave you and your party stranded. You can even crash in the helicopter on the ride up. Skiers and snowboarders have died in all of these ways and more.

But the most common cause of death is by avalanche. Any sound or movement can trigger tons of snow to rush down the mountain at

By the time outside help arrives, it's usually too late for an avalanche victim to survive.

100 miles (160 km) per hour. The avalanche sends bodies tumbling. One survivor describes it as being stuck inside a washing machine filled with rocks. Most people don't escape alive. The wall of snow slams them against trees or rocks, killing them instantly. Or it buries them alive to suffocate within a few minutes.

Big-Wave Surfing

You are 40 feet (12 m) in the air. You are standing barefoot on a surfboard on water. The water is moving fast! You are big-wave surfing!

A wave must be at least 20 feet (6 m) tall to be considered a "big" wave. Surfers compete on waves that are sometimes more than 60 feet (18 m) high. That's as tall as a seven-story building. Surfing in such conditions can be deadly.

How do you get on top of a gigantic wave? You can lie stomach down on your surfboard and paddle onto it. Or you can be towed onto it. This is known as tow surfing. A Jet Ski or helicopter will tow you to the top of a wave. Next thing you know, you're on a 10-foot (3 m) long slippery board with a powerful wave crashing around you.

Jet Ski = a small motorized watercraft

SURF SPEAK!

Here are some words and phrases to know so you feel safe in the water:

- amped = fired up or excited to be surfing
- betty = a girl that surfs
- bomb = a huge wave, also called "hugangus"
- grommet = a young surfer
- men in gray suits = sharks
- rag-dolled = getting tossed by a wave

Big waves generate powerful force. You are at the mercy of the wave. The greatest risk of a big-wave wipeout is getting slammed into the ocean floor. Your neck can snap like a twig. Another risk is drowning. The wave's force can spin you dizzy. Just as you figure which way is up, another wave can pound you back down.

Yet another danger is plunging from the top of the wave to the lowest point. A fall of 60 feet (18 m) or more, even landing in water, isn't safe. Still, these dangers haven't stopped surfers from chasing that next big wave.

Paddling on a surfboard is one way to reach a huge wave.

INDYCAR RACING

You've ridden in a car going 65 miles (105 km) per hour on a highway, right? Now imagine going three times that fast. With no roof. And with cars on both sides of you mere inches away. Traveling at dangerously high speeds like that is a recipe for disaster. That's IndyCar racing.

A race car driver is four times more likely to be killed than a boxer and thirty times more likely than a football player. IndyCar racing is among the most dangerous forms of auto racing. People also call it open-wheel racing. The car's wide tires are out in the open, not hidden beneath its body. The open wheels make any contact with another car potentially disastrous. The famous Indianapolis 500 is held every May at the Indianapolis Motor Speedway. Since the race began in 1909, forty-one drivers have been killed.

RACE CAR FANS IN DANGER

Drivers aren't the only ones in danger at a car race. Fans are in harm's way just by attending the event. Of the thirty-three deadliest sporting events in history, ten have been auto races. All the races included deaths to spectators. In every case, the race car or parts of it flew into the crowd.

The deadliest crash occurred in 1955 at the 24 Hours of Le Mans motor race in France. Driver Pierre Levegh accidentally slammed into another car. Levegh's car somersaulted and broke apart. Car parts hurtled into the stands. The driver and eighty-three spectators were killed.

Racetracks are safer for fans these days. Fences in place to protect fans are made of steel wire mesh. This sturdy material helps prevent flying cars or debris from crashing into the stands.

No track is completely safe, though. The 2011 IndyCar World Championships at Las Vegas Motor Speedway was the scene of a horrific crash. Cars were roaring at 220 miles (354 km) per hour when two of them bumped. This set off a chain reaction. In the next instant, fifteen cars skidded sideways, tumbled upside down, and flew through the air.

Dan Wheldon won the Indy 500 just a few short months before his death.

A gasoline-filled race car in the air is no longer a car—it's a flying bomb! Several cars burst into flames. Dan Wheldon's car flew 325 feet (99 m) in the air—the distance in professional baseball from home plate to some outfield walls. Wheldon's car slammed into a fence. He died instantly of head trauma.

IndyCar racing is getting safer. Drivers wear full-face helmets and fireproof suits. Usually, a driver climbs out of a fiery wreck. But part of the excitement of racing is the danger. And as long as people race, people are going to die.

This driver's helmet and fireproof suit may help protect him if he crashes.

BASEjumper.com
http://www.basejumper.com/
Check out this website to find out what it takes to be a BASE jumper. There are articles from experts, as well as photos and videos of awesome jumps. You can easily create a user name and password to log in.

Cave Diving Website
http://www.cavediving.com
Visit this website to learn what it takes to be a cave diver. The site tells you where the best caves are and how to practice safety when exploring them.

Fightnews.com
http://www.fightnews.com
This website has everything you want to know about boxing. It provides up-to-the-minute news, current rankings of the fighters in every weight class, the complete boxing schedule, and much more.

Hile, Lori. *Surviving Extreme Sports.* Chicago: Heinemann Raintree, 2011. This exciting book tells the story of athletes who survived deep-water dives, steep climbs without a rope, and many other extreme sporting adventures. It includes colorful charts and "Survival Science" boxes.

IndyCar
http://www.indycar.com
This is the official website of the IndyCar racing series. It provides current news of all things racing, biographies of the professional drivers, racing results, and action-packed photos and videos.

Laurendeau, Jason. *BASE Jumping: The Ultimate Guide.* Santa Barbara, CA: Greenwood Publishing Group, 2012. This book is packed with information about how BASE jumping got started, as well as the equipment and techniques used to complete a successful jump. This book features interviews with several jumpers.

Otfinoski, Steven. *Extreme Surfing.* New York: Marshall Cavendish Benchmark, 2012. This book tells the history of surfing and the wild antics of surfing on the edge. It has plenty of colorful photos of surfers in action.

Zuehlke, Jeffrey. *Supercross.* Minneapolis: Lerner Publications Company, 2008. Check out this exciting book about the indoor version of motocross. It describes how riders fly over jumps and sail around turns in a frantic race to the finish line.

INDEX

The images in this book are used with the permission of: © Christoffer Askman/the Agency Collection/Getty Images, p. 4; © Rapsodia/SuperStock, p. 5; AP Photo/George Nikitin, p. 6; © Martin Philbey/Pasadena Star-News/ZUMA Press, p. 7; AP Photo/Jae C. Hong, p. 8; © Nordic Photos/SuperStock, p. 9 (top); © Leemage/UIG via Getty Images, pp. 9 (bottom), 15 (bottom); © Boris Streubel/Bongarts/Getty Images, p. 10 (top); AP Photo/The Canadian Press, Ryan Remiorz, p. 10 (bottom); AP Photo/Eric Jamison, p. 11; © Thomas Bjoernflaten/AFP/Getty Images, p. 12; AP Photo/Darko Vojinovic, p. 13; © Tengku Bahar/AFP/Getty Images, p. 14; © Jeff Swensen/Getty Images, p. 15 (top); © Steve Bloom Images/SuperStock, p. 16; © iStockphoto.com/Berenika Lychak, p. 17 (top); © Luis Sandoval/SuperStock, p. 17 (bottom); © Jeff Gross/Getty Images, p. 18; © Tony Donaldson/Icon SMI, p. 19 (background); © Ian Walton/Getty Images, p. 19 (inset); © Jimmy Chin/National Geographic Society/CORBIS, p. 20; © Corey Rich/ Aurora Open/SuperStock, p. 21 (top); © Travel Library Limited/SuperStock, p. 21 (bottom); © Tony Harrington/StockShot/Alamy, p. 22; © Marc Muench/CORBIS, p. 23 (top); © Ed Darack/Science Faction/SuperStock, p. 23 (bottom); © Pacific Stock - Design Pics/SuperStock, p. 24; © Cavan Images/Taxi/Getty Images, p. 25 (background); © Paul Kennedy/Lonely Planet Images/Getty Images, p. 25 (inset); © Ron Bijlsma/Zuma Press, Inc./Alamy, p. 26; © Jonathan Ferrey/Getty Images, p. 27; © Matt Bolt/Icon SMI, p. 28; © Robert Laberge/Getty Images, p. 29 (top); © Transtock/ SuperStock, p. 29 (bottom).

Front cover: © Empire331/Dreamstime.com.

Main body text set in Calvert MT Std Regular 11/16.
Typeface provided by Monotype Typography.